GET TO KNOW ANIMALS ... of the FOREST

The Center for Science Teaching and Learning

Get To Know Animals of the Forest
Copyright © 2021 by The Center for Science Teaching and Learning
All rights reserved
Illustrations by Ellen Valentino
Published by Red Penguin Books
Bellerose Village, New York
Library of Congress Control Number: 2021912889
ISBN
Print 978-1-63777-096-2/978-1-63777-097-9
Digital 978-1-63777-098-6
No part of this book may be reproduced in any form or by any electronic or mechanical means, including information storage and retrieval systems, without written permission from the author, except for the use of brief quotations in a book review.

Animals are amazing! They live all over the world and they all look very different from one another. Some are plant eaters, some are meat eaters, and some eat both! But do you know what a female, male, baby and a group of each type of animal is called? Many animals have different names for each and some are very interesting while some are really funny!

A forest is a piece of land with many trees. Many animals need forests to live and survive. Forests are very important and grow in many places around the world. Most forests have evergreen trees and also have very few bushes and other smaller plants.

Eagle

Bald eagles and golden eagles are found in North America.

Where they live: There are many species of eagle. Eagles live on every continent except Antarctica. Golden eagles can also be found in Europe and Asia.

Types of environment: Near rivers, lakes, and beaches (bald eagles), open woodlands and on cliffsides near open plains (golden eagles).

Diet: Bald eagles mostly eat fish. They also steal food from smaller birds. Golden eagles hunt rabbits, squirrels, smaller birds, tortoises, and sometimes even animals as large as baby goats. They wait until they see a goat climbing a cliff, then they swoop down at high speed, latch onto the goat's back, and try to drag it off the cliff side. Sometimes they succeed.

What Do You Call ...

a male eagle?
Male

a female eagle?
Female

a baby eagle?
Eaglet

a group of eagles?
Convocation

Fox

The largest and most common fox in North America is the red fox.

Where they live: Foxes live on every continent except Antarctica. They were introduced to Australia by hunters in the 1800s where they have since become an invasive species.

Types of environment: Wide variety of habitats, from forests and plains to arctic tundra.

Diet: Foxes are mostly carnivorous and predatory, hunting animals smaller than themselves such as rabbits, rodents, and fish. Like bears, sometimes they will eat fruit. Foxes in cities are known to dig through human garbage.

What Do You Call ...

a male fox?
Dog

a female fox?
Vixen

a baby fox?
Cub, Pup or Kit

a group of foxes?
Skulk or Pack

Hawk
Hawks are clever, medium-sized hunters.

Where they live: North America, Central America, and Jamaica. Red-tailed hawks are the most common hawk in North America and live in grasslands and woodlands.

Types of environment: On the forest's edge, near open fields.

Diet: Red-tailed hawks eat mice, rats, squirrels, and other rodents, as well as rabbits and hares. They will also attack ground birds such as pheasants, and sometimes even eat snakes and already dead animals.

What Do You Call ...

a male hawk?
Tiercel

a female hawk?
Hen

a baby hawk?
Eyas

a group of hawks?
Cast

Hummingbird

Among the most common hummingbirds in eastern and central North America are ruby-throated hummingbirds.

Where they live: Hummingbirds are restricted to North and South America.

Types of environment: Open woodlands with abundant flowers, nectar, and tree sap.

Diet: Hummingbirds need to eat energy-rich food such as sugary nectar to power their flight and keep their bodies warm. Baby hummingbirds also eat insects for the extra protein required to grow. Hummingbirds have long, thin bills and tongues to reach inside flowers for nectar, and can beat their wings so quickly they are able to hover in mid-air.

What Do You Call ...

a male hummingbird?
Cock

a baby hummingbird?
Chick

a female hummingbird?
Hen

a group of hummingbirds?
Charm

Mallard

Mallards are one of the most familiar of all of the ducks.

Where they live: Mallards can be found in North America, southern Greenland, Europe, and Asia.

Types of environment: Wetlands and temperate forests, generally around bodies of freshwater. Mallards are adaptable around humans, able to thrive in neighborhoods and parks with large ponds.

Diet: Mallards eat all kinds of things that live in and around freshwater. This includes aquatic insect larvae, worms, snails, centipedes, small fish and tadpoles. They also eat grass, and aquatic plants such as duckweed. During migration, they mostly eat grass, seeds, and sometimes human crops such as wheat.

What Do You Call ...

a male mallard?
Drake

a female mallard?
Duck

a baby mallard?
Duckling

a group of mallards?
Sord or Flock

Owl

Owls have feathers that are made for silent flying so they can surprise their prey.

Where they live: Every continent except Antarctica. A barn owl's wings are lined along the front edge with sound-absorbing fluff that allows them to fly silently. Their ears are extremely sensitive. One ear is located higher on the head than the other one; this difference gives them a greater ability to compare and locate very quiet sounds, like the sound of a mouse moving under deep snow.

Types of environment: Wide variety of habitats from dense forests and mixed woodlands to open plains and tundra.

Diet: Smaller owls eat insects, small birds, and mammals such as mice. Larger owls may eat smaller owls, other birds, and larger mammals such as rats and rabbits.

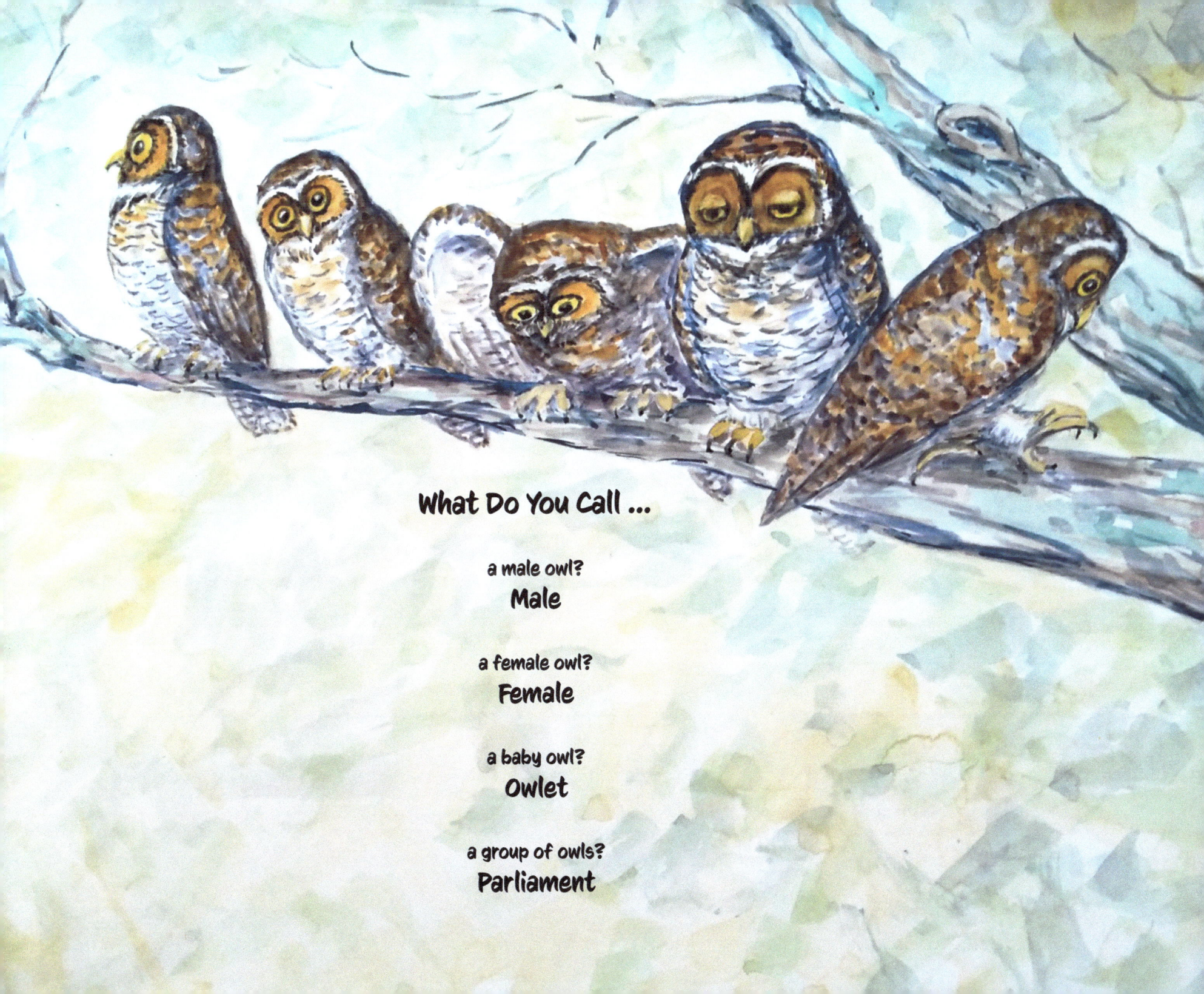

What Do You Call ...

a male owl?
Male

a female owl?
Female

a baby owl?
Owlet

a group of owls?
Parliament

Porcupine

Porcupines protect themselves with a coat of long, sharp quills.

Where they live: Different types of porcupines inhabit North America, Africa and the Amazon rainforest. The prehensile-tailed porcupine of the Amazon rainforest can curl its tail around tree branches like a monkey.

Type of environment: Forests in North America, deserts and plains in sub-Saharan Africa, and rainforests in the Amazon of South America.

Diet: Porcupines mostly eat things on the ground, including leaves, shoots, berries and other fruits, nuts, grass, bark, conifer needles, roots, bulbs, and occasionally small animals. The prehensile-tailed porcupine will venture further into trees.

What Do You Call ...

a male porcupine?
Boar

a female porcupine?
Sow

a baby porcupine?
Pup

a group of porcupines?
Prickle or Family

Rabbit

A rabbit's teeth never stop growing, which means they have to chew and chew to wear them down.

Where they live: There are around 80 species of lagomorphs (rabbits, hares, pikas) found everywhere on Earth except the West Indies, southern parts of South America, Madagascar, several islands of southeast Asia, and Antarctica.

Types of environment: Open, grassy environments such as grasslands, semi-arid deserts, and tundra. Rabbits will dig burrows in the ground to sleep, hide, and raise their babies.

Diet: Rabbits eat grass and low shrubs.

What Do You Call ...

a male rabbit?
Buck

a female rabbit?
Doe

a baby rabbit?
Bunny

a group of rabbits?
Nest, Warren, or Colony

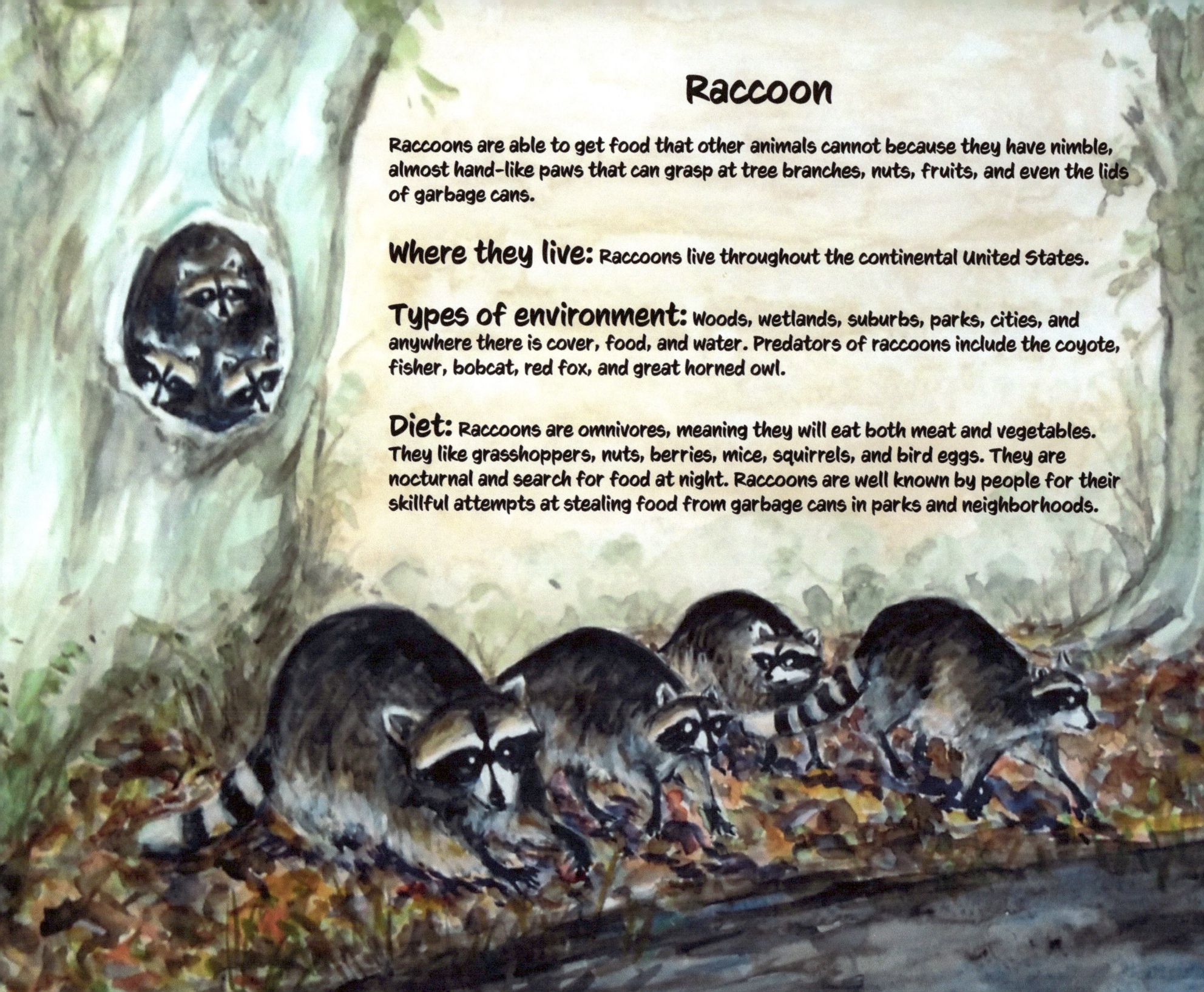

Raccoon

Raccoons are able to get food that other animals cannot because they have nimble, almost hand-like paws that can grasp at tree branches, nuts, fruits, and even the lids of garbage cans.

Where they live: Raccoons live throughout the continental United States.

Types of environment: Woods, wetlands, suburbs, parks, cities, and anywhere there is cover, food, and water. Predators of raccoons include the coyote, fisher, bobcat, red fox, and great horned owl.

Diet: Raccoons are omnivores, meaning they will eat both meat and vegetables. They like grasshoppers, nuts, berries, mice, squirrels, and bird eggs. They are nocturnal and search for food at night. Raccoons are well known by people for their skillful attempts at stealing food from garbage cans in parks and neighborhoods.

What Do You Call ...

a male raccoon?
Boar

a baby raccoon?
Kit

a female raccoon?
Sow

a group of raccoons?
Gaze